Goodnight Toes!

*Bedtime Stories, Lullabies,
and Movement Games*

By Anne Lief Barlin

BOOKS   Hello Toes! Movement Games for Children
                 (with Nurit Kalev)
                 Creative Babies
                 Dance-a-Story
                 The Art of Learning Through Movement
                 Dance-a-Folk Song
                 Teaching Your Wings to Fly
                 Move and Be Moved *(with Tamara Greenberg)*

RECORDS /
CASSETTES   Goodnight Toes! Cassette *(with Marcia Berman)*
                 Hello Toes! Cassette *(with Marcia Berman)*
                 Rainy Day Dances: Rainy Day Songs
                 (with Patty Zeitlin and Marcia Berman)
                 Dance-a-Story: Sing-a-Song *(with Marcia Berman)*
                 Cloud Journeys *(with Marcia Berman)*

FILMS /
VIDEOS   Learning Through Movement
                 Esther Dances Helen Keller
                 Teaching Your Wings to Fly
                 Kibbutz Exercises for Vatikim
                 Movement Games for Adults with Children

Goodnight Toes!

Bedtime Stories, Lullabies, and Movement Games

Anne Lief Barlin and Nurit Kalev

A Dance Horizons Book
Princeton Book Company, Publishers

Text photographs are by Vivienne Silver and Roy Brody © 1993 except for those on pages 7, 9, 16, 22, 63, 113, and 118, which are supplied by Tamagawa University, Japan.

A Dance Horizons Book
Princeton Book Company, Publishers
P. O. Box 57
Pennington, NJ 08534

Cover drawing copyright © by Deirdre Sheean
Interior design by Anne O'Donnell based upon the design by Roxanne Barrett of Hello Toes! Movement Games for Children.

Library of Congress Cataloging-in-Publication Data

Barlin, Anne Lief.
   Goodnight toes! : bedtime stories, lullabies, and movement games /
Anne Lief Barlin and Nurit Kalev.
        p.   cm.
   "A Dance Horizons book."
   ISBN 0-87127-190-7
   1. Movement education-—Study and teaching (Preschool) 2. Movement
education—Study and teaching (Elementary) 3. Dancing for children--Study and
teaching (Preschool) 4. Dancing for children-—Study and teaching (Elementary) 5.
Creative ability in children. I. Kalev, Nurit. II. Title.
GV452.B363 1993
372.86-—dc20   93-8560

Contents

Foreword

If you believe as I do that every child has a right to a childhood with dance, music, and art at its center and that each child needs to learn to function as a cooperative and loving member of society, then it follows that movement and creative activities that bring children and their families together are at the starting point—they're the beginning of building a sound foundation with dance and creativity at its core. And it will serve us well.

Goodnight Toes! and its creators Anne Barlin and Nurit Kalev give us the building blocks to use. Parents and children that delve into these pages will happily receive new skills and enduring values to last a lifetime.

MARCIA BERMAN
Composer, Singer,
Producer, B/B Records

Preface

● How to Use This Book

Goodnight Toes! can of course be read cover to cover, if you so wish. You will find it is most beneficial as a resource book to be used again and again with children from ages three to ten, relieving their pent-up tensions and stretching their minds and bodies. Explore the text, experiment with different activities, and develop your own variations and interpretations of these dance games.

However, each activity should be read in its entirety before presenting it to children. You will need to learn whether music is required at all; whether it is needed to introduce the activity or whether it comes later. At the beginning of each activity where accompaniment is required, songs from the *Goodnight Toes! Cassette* are listed. Necessary supplies—common household items or easily obtainable toys—are announced at the outset. Many of the games require active imaginations only. Instructions to you alone are indicated with the heading *ADULT*. The suggested script to be read to the children while leading the activity follows the heading *CHILDREN*.

▲ About Musical Accompaniment

We have prepared the *Goodnight Toes! Cassette* to accompany the dance and movement games in this book. The contents of the cassette are as follows:

Side One—All the Pretty Horses; Russian Lullabye; Pajamas; Goodnight Song; Sleep Songs; Hit the Road to Dreamland; Raisins and Almonds

Side Two—Goodnight Toes; Listening Music, Classical Style; Dancing Marionette; Learning to Skip; Sprightly Rhythms; Rhythm Game; Greensleeves; Learning to Gallop; Trains and Stations

You may find that using this tape will give you some good ideas from which you can experiment further with music in your own collection or from your local library. We've indicated in the text where on the cassette the accompanying music is located. An order form for the purchase of the cassette appears at the end of this book.

■ Music or Silence?

Moving to music and moving in silence are both extremely valuable.

Music establishes and enhances a magical atmosphere, one that takes children out of their everyday existence. Music teaches about other cultures, other sounds, other rhythms. It widens vistas and helps to teach respect and appreciation of other peoples.

Music acts as an authority, helping to discipline listeners. When children follow musical cues, when they respond to emotional cues inherent in music, they are taught by music. You have relegated the authority to the music; it is no longer you instructing the children. The music is now their teacher.

When music is not present to influence their movement, children are more likely to become aware of their own feelings. Music demands interpretation. Silence helps children to focus inward. Silence forces them to listen more closely to their body's responses—their tensions, their energy levels, their breathing, their placement. When music or other outside elements are not present, it's possible to become more and more aware of one's feelings.

Silence helps when working with a partner. As children become more and more aware of their partners, they connect on a deeper and deeper level. This process encourages an extension of their attention span.

Children cannot be expected to engage in silent activity for long, but when each partner is encouraged to focus on the other, unexpected benefits are revealed.

You will find many exercises in this book that can be done with the *Goodnight Toes! Cassette* or without music. Try doing them one way some of the time; the other way another time.

● Why Do Children Need to Relax?

Most of us live in a world full of stress. We are always in a hurry. There is never enough time. Many of our children have absorbed and internalized the intense, speeded-up rhythms of our lives.

Helping children to relax their bodies gives them the gift of time. When children let go in their muscles, when they stop to count the rhythm of their breathing, the blood is allowed to flow freely to and from their brain.

As a result, they can think.

They can become aware of what is being said to them.

They can hear clearly.

They can observe carefully.

They can absorb.

▲ Ask Questions: Teaching Children to Think

Asking children movement questions, such as "Can you create a round shape when you stretch the elastic?" from Part Three: Movement Games Using Objects, motivates them to visualize a movement in order to formulate a verbal response. When children are doing the movement, listening to the question and finding their answers, they are thinking. It is this thinking process that integrates the right and left hemispheres of the brain.

It is fascinating to observe children gaining an understanding and internalizing some extremely adult concepts. They are learning by means of a thinking process that is rarely encouraged.

■ Let Them Perform for One Another

All parents and teachers know that children love to perform. Often we have called them little hams.

There are children who refuse to perform—and we wish they were less shy.

There are children who overdo it—and we wish they would stop.

But somewhere in between, there seems to be a healthy need.

A need to share with others what is uniquely ours.

A need to feel accepted for that sharing by the adult world and by one's peers.

So encourage children to perform. Their increased confidence will be your reward.

PART ONE:
Bedtime Stories, Lullabies, and Rhythmic Chants

All the Pretty Horses

WHAT YOUR CHILDREN WILL GAIN FROM THIS EXPERIENCE		

PHYSICAL / MUSICAL
Balance
Integration of Movement
  & Music
Body / Voice
  Coordination
	COGNITIVE
	Integration of
	  Movement &
	  Language
		EMOTIONAL / SOCIAL
		Expression of Tender
		  Feelings
		Relaxation

ACCOMPANIMENT
"All the Pretty Horses" SIDE A, TRACK 1

● You Need

A stuffed animal or doll for each child.

ADULT

Allow the young children to do the gallop step in any way that they can. The major intent of this dance is to encourage the gentle, tender connection that the children are making with their "baby." However, for older children (over ages five or six), and only after they have learned the dance and can express their feelings, teach them the skill of galloping. Look for "Learning to Gallop" on page 106.

This activity could be (but need not be) introduced with The Magic Basket on page 18.

CHILDREN

You are helping your "baby" to fall asleep. Put your baby on the floor in front of you. Stand. Be sure to make enough space so that "the pretty little horses" will have enough room to gallop around your baby.

● Song

Hush you by, don't you cry

Go to sleepy, little baby

● Movement

With open arms, look down at your baby.

Sing and sway from side to side.

When you wake, you shall have
All the pretty little horses

Do a pony gallop around your own baby.

Blacks and bays, dapples and grays

Repeat the sway from side to side.

Coach and six little horses

Repeat the pony gallop around your baby. Your baby is now asleep.

Hush you by, don't you cry

Quietly go down on your knees.

Go to sleepy, little baby

Very gently, pick up your baby. Sit. Put your finger to your lips and whisper, "Shhhh . . . "

The Sleepy Bear

WHAT YOUR CHILDREN WILL GAIN FROM THIS EXPERIENCE		
PHYSICAL / MUSICAL *Slow Warm-Up* *Toes Stretch* *Full Body Stretch* *Body Control* *Relaxation*	*COGNITIVE* *Integration of* * Movement &* *Language*	*EMOTIONAL / SOCIAL* *Music from Another* * Culture*

ACCOMPANIMENT
"Russian Lullabye" SIDE A, TRACK 2
"Listening Music" SIDE B, TRACK 2

▲ Sleeping Bear Story

ADULT   Speak slowly and quietly. Wait for each child to complete each action.

CHILDREN   You know that bears hibernate—they curl up and sleep all winter long.

               You be the bear. Lie down and curl up to keep yourself warm. You have been sleeping all winter. Spring is almost here.

▲ Stretching Bear

CHILDREN   You feel very lazy. Slowly and carefully, stretch one arm way out in front of you.

               Now stretch the arm to the side.

               Now stretch it behind you.

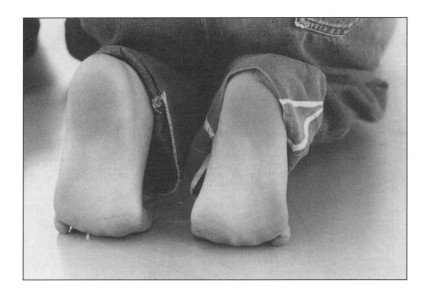

Now stretch the other arm forward, to the side, and to the back.

Slowly roll onto your hands and knees.

Tuck all of your toes under you so you are on the balls of your feet.

Press the floor with both hands.

Rock slowly forward and backward four times.

Rock as far backward as you possibly can so that you can feel your toes stretching. You are helping your feet to wake up.

Keep both hands on the floor. Lift one knee and slowly stretch the leg backward.

Bend the knee and place it back down to the floor.

Give the other leg a turn to stretch.

Stretch each leg four times.

Lie on your stomach.

Stretch both arms long in front of you and stretch both legs long behind you at the same time.

Keep stretching both your arms and legs while I count: One, two, three, four.

ADULT   Count only as long as your children can tolerate the stretch. Then lower the lights—just slightly. Avoid total darkness. Let them relax and just listen to some quiet music.

Dancing Marionette

WHAT YOUR CHILDREN WILL GAIN FROM THIS EXPERIENCE		
PHYSICAL / MUSICAL *Body Control* *Isolation of Body Parts* *Flexibility* *Relaxation*	*COGNITIVE* *Naming Body Parts*	*EMOTIONAL / SOCIAL* *Imagination* *Ingenuity* *Relaxation* *Flexibility*

ACCOMPANIMENT
"Dancing Marionette" SIDE B, TRACK 3
"Sleep Songs" SIDE A, TRACK 5
"Goodnight Song" SIDE A, TRACK 4
"Listening Music" SIDE B, TRACK 2
"Russian Lullabye" SIDE A, TRACK 2

ADULT   Put on the accompanying music. If you would like the children to remain resting on the floor after the "Dancing Marionette" music has ended, play one of the quiet, peaceful selections suggested above.

CHILDREN   You are a marionette. The puppeteer is sitting on the ceiling holding you up.

Let me see how the strings lift your wrists, your elbows, your head, your back, your knees, your toes, your stomach, your nose.

The puppeteer says, I like this marionette. I like the way you can move in so many directions. I'm going to make you dance.

Look at the funny way your arms are swinging.

I like the way your head is bouncing around. And your legs—they're lifting forward and backward and sideways.

And your back—it's bending and twisting.

And your toes—they're jiggling. Gosh, this is fun!

Oh, oh! Something's happened!

The string on your head just broke!

Drop your head. It can't move any more.

But all of the other strings are still pulling.

Your legs are still bouncing.

Your knees and elbows are lifting.

Your back is moving.

Oh, oh, more strings are broken! Now your arms and your head are hanging down. They can't move.

But your back and legs are still bouncing!

Your knees are dancing. Your feet are jumping.

Your back is loose and happy and bobbing around.

Oh, oh, now the string on your back is broken.

Only your legs can still move!

Your legs are swinging forward and backward.

Your feet are dancing.

Your knees are bouncing.

Oh, oh, the strings on your legs are broken!

What can you do? Lie down flat on your back while I walk around to see everybody's broken strings. Let's give this poor, tired marionette a good rest.

Goodnight Toes

WHAT YOUR CHILDREN WILL GAIN FROM THIS EXPERIENCE		
PHYSICAL / MUSICAL	COGNITIVE	EMOTIONAL / SOCIAL
Locating & Exercising Many Parts of the Body	Verbal & Body Coordination	Expressing Emotions Through the Body
Exploring New Ways of Using the Body	Naming Body Parts	Imagination
Feeling Rhythm Through the bBdy	Integrating Both Hemispheres of the Brain	Relaxation
Relaxation		Confidence
		Feeling Part of the Group

ACCOMPANIMENT
"Goodnight Toes" SIDE B, TRACK 1

■ You Need

Bare feet.

Adult participation.

ADULT   The children will learn to chant along with you and with the tape, and they will gradually pick up on the rhythmic flow in the same way that they enjoy the flow of a song. Chanting with a whole group adds a good deal of physical and emotional gratification.

● Chant

Good Morning Toes

Goodnight Toes

● Movement

Briskly flex your feet from your ankles so that your toes are pointing toward the ceiling.

Totally relax your ankles. Release all of the tension out of your feet. Let your toes feel droopy.

11

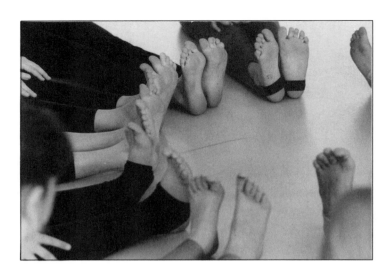

Good Morning Toes
Goodnight Toes
Good Morning Toes
*My toes are playing
all day long.*

Flex your feet.

Relax your feet.

Flex your feet.

Move only from the ankles.
Dance your feet happily in all
directions.

And now *they feel*	Release the tension one foot at a time.
very	Relax the toes,
very *sleepy.*	then very slowly let the energy flow out of the ankles.
Good Morning Hands	Briskly bring your hands in front of you and brightly look at your palms.
Goodnight Hands	Relax and turn your wrists so that your palms are facing the floor.
Good Morning Hands	Briskly turn your hands to look brightly at your palms.
Goodnight Hands	Relax and turn your wrists.
Good Morning Hands	Briskly turn your hands to look brightly at your palms.
My hands are playing *all day long.*	From the wrists, dance your hands happily in all directions. Keep your arms in front of you.
And now *they feel* *very* *very* *sleepy.*	Release the energy separately from each wrist. Turn each hand until the palm is facing the floor. Keep your arms in front of you. Let your fingers droop so that the wrist is clearly pointing to the ceiling.
Good Morning Arms	Briskly lift both arms in front of you. Look at them as though seeing them for the first time.
Goodnight Arms	Relax and let both arms drop to your sides.
Good Morning Arms	Briskly lift both arms in front of you.
Goodnight Arms	Relax both arms.
Good Morning Arms	Briskly lift both arms.

My arms are playing all day long.	Swing your arms happily and freely in all directions.
And now they feel	Gradually release the energy from one arm at a time.
very	Let the fingers droop.
very	Let the hand droop.
sleepy.	Let the whole arm relax from the shoulder and slowly lower to your side.

ADULT   Ask the children to suggest other parts of the body and other ways in which those parts can be "playing all day long" and how they can be "very, very sleepy." And then instruct them to let all of those parts get very, very sleepy.

CHILDREN   What other parts of your body can you wake up? Your shoulders? Your elbows? Your knees? How about your face? Your tongue? And then let all of those parts get very, very sleepy.

Learning to Skip

WHAT YOUR CHILDREN WILL GAIN FROM THIS EXPERIENCE		

PHYSICAL/MUSICAL
Coordination
Body Control
Use of Nondominant
  Side
Responding to Rhythm
Coordinating Rhythm &
  Movement
	COGNITIVE
	Problem Solving
	Conscious Muscle
	  Control
		EMOTIONAL/SOCIAL
		Self-Esteem
		Confidence
		Measuring up to One's
		  Peers
		Joy

ACCOMPANIMENT
"Learning to Skip" SIDE B, TRACK 4

ADULT

When the child is still struggling with the process of learning to skip, it is best to avoid the music.

When the child has achieved the ability to keep each knee to the ball while hopping, then the music can be very helpful. But at first, do the skip in half-time as the capitalized words indicate.

When the skip has clearly been accomplished, double the rhythm of the movement, so that the child is now skipping freely and happily.

CHILDREN

One day I was at the beach
playing with my friend.
I threw a beach ball to my friend.
She caught it. But it was a very windy day.
So when she threw the ball back to me, it went
over my head and into the water.
I picked up the ball and said,
"Mr. Beach Ball, please don't go into the water any
more because if I get wet on such a windy day,
My mother will make me go home

and I want to stay and play, okay?"
Do you think the beach ball heard me?
Maybe we'll find out later in the story.

So I threw the ball again
and she caught it just fine.
But this time the wind was much stronger.
When she threw it, it blew
way over my head
and went farther out in the water
and I got much wetter.
I said to the ball,
"Now look here, Mr. Beach Ball,
I told you not to go into the water.
I'm cold now and I'm angry
and I feel like giving you a spanking!"

Should I spank him?
"Well, I think I'll give you another chance.
But only one more chance.
Remember that."

So I threw the ball again.
This time, the wind was so strong
it was almost a hurricane! The ball went
way, way over my head and
far, far out into the water.
I got very wet
and very mad! And I said,
"This is it! I told you what would happen if you went
into the water again!"

You know, I think the beach ball really heard me.
It kept trying to jump out of my arms.
Or maybe it was the wind blowing so hard.
I had to hold it—with both arms—very firmly.
(Do you know what "firmly" means? Yes, "tightly.")
How could I spank him if I can't use my hands?
Use my head? My nose? My knees? Yes! With my
knees!

First	one knee	and then	the other.
SPANK,	SPANK,	SPANK,	SPANK!
Each	knee	gets	a turn.
SPANK,	SPANK,	SPANK,	SPANK!
First	one knee	and then	the other.
SPANK,	SPANK,	SPANK,	SPANK!

Oh-oh, I hear another voice—
it's the sound of the wind.
It's talking to me. It says,
"Hang on tightly. Keep lifting each knee
high to the ball.
I'll blow you both
high to the sky.
I'll teach you to skip!"

The WIND is BLOWing me UP to the SKY.
I'm SKIPping and SKIPping and EACH knee is HIGH.
The WIND is BLOWing us BOTH to the SKY.
We're SKIPping and SKIPping
          and EACH knee is HIGH.
I'm HOLDing you FIRMly, we're LEARNing to FLY.
We're SKIPping and SKIPping way UP to the SKY.

The Magic Basket

ADULT　　　Here is a story that you will find extremely useful for introducing any movement activity that requires imagining some object or animal that the children will be moving with. They love the story and will listen with rapt attention. The key to their attentiveness is your own dramatic involvement. The basket can contain animals or balloons or whatever else you want them to imagine moving with that day.

● Story

CHILDREN　Every time I come to class, I bring a magic basket! It's a very big, round basket, so let's make a big circle around it.
What makes it magic is that I never know what I will find inside. Every time I open it, I find something else. Would you like to see what's in the magic basket today?

ADULT　　　Move toward the center of the room. Use both arms. Pretend to lift open two huge doors.

CHILDREN

I see a baby bear and a kitten and an elephant. What else do I see?

ADULT　　　Walk around inside of the circle pointing to the floor in front of each child as you progress. Imagine that you are really seeing the animal. Point to the floor, look at the child, and wait expectantly for an answer. If the child needs help, make a suggestion and go on to the next child until they've each had a turn.

Everyone, cover your eyes with your hands and think what kind of an animal you would like best. You can choose any kind of animal, even if someone has chosen the same kind as yours. Thee are so many animals in this basket, you can't even count them. That's what makes it magic!

Now open your eyes. Don't tell what you have chosen. It's a secret.

When I come around to you, whisper the secret into my ear.

ADULT   Have each child whisper in your ear so that her or his choice is clearly a secret. Then walk to the center of the circle and "lift" the requested item from the basket. The children will be absorbed in watching the way in which you lift and carry. If a child has asked for a hippopotamus for instance, pretend to lift a hippopotamus from the basket, exaggerating its weight and size and the difficulty you are having carrying the load. Each "secret" will have its own possibility for an amusing interpretation on your part. Have fun with it. They will love you for it.

When all of the children have received their requests, any or all of the following movement lessons can begin: All the Pretty Horses on page 2; Pajamas on page 20; Magic Balloons on page 100.

Pajamas

WHAT YOUR CHILDREN WILL GAIN FROM THIS EXPERIENCE		
PHYSICAL / MUSICAL	COGNITIVE	EMOTIONAL / SOCIAL
Tempo	Integration of	Imagination
Syncopation	Movement &	Freedom to Improvise
	Language	Confidence
	Contrast	Alertness
		Self-Esteem
		Fun

ACCOMPANIMENT
"Pajamas" SIDE A, TRACK 3
"Sleep Songs" SIDE A, TRACK 5

▲ You Need

Real clothing from your supply of dress-up clothes or pajamas or imaginary brand-new pajamas from the Magic Basket (see page 18).

An audience of children, if done in a group, or stuffed animals or dolls or an imaginary audience.

▲ Proud Walk

ADULT

After you and the children have donned real or imagined pajamas, put on the accompanying music. Let the rhythmic pulse of the music flow through your body. Feel free to clap your hands or sway in place. Dance around the room, stepping and clapping as you enjoy the syncopation of the music. The children will begin to imitate some of your movements. Encourage their participation and individuality with such comments as "How beautiful you look in your new pajamas!" and "I love the way you are dancing to the music!"

As you move around the room, observe how each child is responding and point out the individual interpretations to the music—no matter how simple: "Yes, swing your arms with your body—that's lovely!" "Your head is bobbing right in time with the music!"

After two playings of the music, the children may feel free enough to perform movement in front of an audience.

Ask one of the children to dance for the group and form a large circle of the other children to sit, watch, and enjoy.

There should be no coercion to perform for the class. Sometimes it's easier for children to improvise in groups of two or three. If the group is not ready to move individually in front of an audience, just ask everyone to get up once again and improvise as a group.

Sleep Songs

WHAT YOUR CHILDREN WILL GAIN FROM THIS EXPERIENCE		
PHYSICAL / MUSICAL *Full Body Relaxation* *Locating, Isolating &* *Relaxation Individual* *Body Parts*	*COGNITIVE* *Naming of Individual* *Body Parts*	*EMOTIONAL / SOCIAL* *Release of Stress*

ACCOMPANIMENT
"Sleep Songs" SIDE A, TRACK 5

ADULT

This relaxation game can be played whenever you feel the need.

It can also be used to complete other games, such as Pillow Rest.

CHILDREN

Lie on your back.

Listen to the music. The music tells you which part of your body is falling asleep.

ADULT	When you have turned on the music, lower the lights slightly. Do not allow complete darkness.

Repeat each line of the song in the language most familiar to the children. "Sleep Songs" is sung in Spanish, Japanese, and English on the accompanying *Goodnight Toes! Cassette*. It is valuable for the children to hear a foreign language and then to hear your translation. Their ears will become accustomed to the different sounds.

The tempo of the music allows ample time for your repetitions. Speak as quietly and softly as you can.

The sequence of parts of the body named on *Goodnight Toes! Cassette* is head; arms; legs; eyes; mouth; ears.

■ Song

Let your head fall asleep

Hmm, hmm

Let your arms fall asleep

Hmm, hmm

Let your legs fall asleep

Hmm, hmm

Let your eyes fall asleep

La la la, la la la, la la la, la la la

Let your mouth fall asleep

Hmm, hmm

Let your ears fall asleep

Hmm, hmm

Sleeeeeeeep

Sleeeeeeeep

PART TWO:
Movement Games
Using Objects

Balloons

WHAT YOUR CHILDREN WILL GAIN FROM THIS EXPERIENCE		

PHYSICAL / MUSICAL
Balance / Centering
Body Control of Muscles
  & Joints
Laterality
Response to Music
Quality
Spatial Awareness
Full Body Stretch
	COGNITIVE
	Problem Solving
	Awareness of Time
	Verbal Expression
	Awareness of Shape &
	  Relative Sizes
	Ability to Organize
	Motor Planning
		EMOTIONAL / SOCIAL
		Relaxation
		Attentiveness
		Focus
		Release of Fear
		Closed Eyes
		Relating
		Music Interpretation
		Imagination

● You Need

A deflated medium-sized round balloon of any color for each participant.

ADULT — The balloon lies flat on the floor. Ask your child (or children) the following questions. Be sure to allow them thinking time before answering.

CHILDREN — What is this?

What color is it?

What is it made of?

Why is it flat?

What does it need to make it round?

ADULT — Blow a small amount of air into it. Hold the shape.

CHILDREN — Is it round now?

What did I blow into the balloon?

Is it big or small?

How will it get bigger?

ADULT	Blow more. Hold the new shape.
CHILDREN	Is it bigger now? Would you like me to make it bigger?
ADULT	Blow more. Hold.
CHILDREN	If I keep blowing, what will happen? That's right. But let's keep playing with it. How do I make it smaller?
ADULT	Let out some of the air. Hold.
CHILDREN	Can I make it even smaller?
ADULT	Let out more air. Hold.
CHILDREN	And smaller?

ADULT	Let out more air. Hold.
CHILDREN	How can I make it flat again?
ADULT	Press the balloon flat on the floor.

● Balloon Balance

ADULT	Inflate the balloon and tie a knot in it.
CHILDREN	Can you balance the balloon on the palm of your hand? As you walk? On one finger? On your head? On your stomach? Lying down? How else can you balance the balloon?

● Balloon Snake

CHILDREN	Pass the balloon from one part of your body to another.
	Touch each part and roll it gently to another.

Make no sound, like a snake moving quietly, softly, smoothly.

Roll the balloon around your legs, your arms, your neck, your face. Roll it slowly with the music.

Sit on the floor. Roll the balloon around your feet. Where else can you roll it?

Lie on the floor. How else can you roll the balloon? On your back? On your stomach?

● Balloon Gift

ACCOMPANIMENT
"Listening Music" SIDE B, TRACK 2

CHILDREN   Let's sit get in a circle. The balloon is a beautiful gift that you are presenting to a very good friend.
Pass the balloon to the person next to you, imagining that you are presenting a beautiful gift.

Find your own way of presenting it. Listen to the music. Find your own way of receiving it.

Can you pass it with your eyes closed?

● Time Balloon

ACCOMPANIMENT
"Listening Music" SIDE B, TRACK 2

ADULT   You want the children to become aware of the fact that it takes time for the balloon to return to the ground.

CHILDREN   Toss the balloon high into the air.

Count out loud as the balloon descends.

When the balloon came down, did it drop like a ball?

How many counts did it take before it landed?

Show me how it looked when it was floating down.

Repeat the toss and counting until you have found the best way to get the balloon to float down as slowly as possible.

When I toss it up this time, lift your arms and body up high. Watch the balloon and smoothly dance your way down. I will count to five—try to land only when I have finished counting. One. two, three, four, five.

● Balloon Stretch

ADULT   If you are doing this alone with one child, sit close together and face each other. In a full group, sit together in a close circle.

CHILDREN   Pass the balloon from one person to the next, until it has gone around the whole circle.

Move backward to enlarge the circle.

Again pass the balloon but in the other direction until it is passed completely around the circle.

Is this getting harder?

Again move backward, making the circle even

larger. Staying in the large circle, get on your stomach and stretch your legs out and stretch your arms to pass the balloon around the circle. Keep alternating the direction of the ball.

Is this getting a little harder?

ADULT

Enlarge the circle as much as possible without losing the ability to pass the balloon.

Repeat the whole exercise with the children's backs to the center of the circle. They end by lying on their backs as they try to pass the balloon.

NOTE: For additional activities with balloons, see *Hello Toes!* on pages 3-7.

Blanket

WHAT YOUR CHILDREN WILL GAIN FROM THIS EXPERIENCE		
PHYSICAL / MUSICAL Tactile Sensing Foot Articulation Flexibility Body Control Balance Relaxation	*COGNITIVE* Measuring Concentration Organization Motor Planning Naming of Body Parts	*EMOTIONAL / SOCIAL* Patience Confidence Balance Flexibility Relaxation Fun

ACCOMPANIMENT
"Listening Music" SIDE B, TRACK 2
"Hit the Road to Dreamland" SIDE A, TRACK 6

▲ You Need

One soft blanket for each child or for a small group. For a large group, you will need more than one blanket.

▲ Smooth Blanket

CHILDREN   Place the blanket on the floor.

Stretch it out smoothly.

Walk on top of it without making any wrinkles.

▲ Wrinkled & Smooth

ADULT   Make this a playful game. You will need to help the younger children by doing the smoothing for them after each time that they have done the wrinkling.

CHILDREN   With only your feet, wrinkle the blanket and make it as small as you can.

What a naughty blanket! I will not be able to keep warm if my blanket is so wrinkled! Let's smooth it out.

Smooth the blanket out again. Wrinkle then smooth the blanket with different parts of your body: your elbow, your knee, your buttocks, your head.

▲ Sliding Blanket

CHILDREN   The blanket is smooth on the floor.

Stand next to it with your toes on the edge of the blanket.

Grasp the blanket tightly with your toes, curling the blanket under your toes.

Walk backward to make the blanket slide along the floor.

▲ Blanket Roll

ADULT   Roll up the blanket so that it looks like a rolled-up sleeping bag. An older child may be able to roll the blanket alone.

CHILDREN   Walk on top of the blanket from one end to the other.

Can you balance like a tight-rope walker?

Can you also balance walking backward?

Jump over the blanket roll.

▲ Blanket Rest

CHILDREN   On your stomach, stretch the whole length of your body on top of the blanket. It is time for a rest.

ADULT   At this point, turn on the music.

Grasp one end of one child's blanket roll. The rest of the children will be lying quietly on their blanket rolls, listening to the music.

Walk backward, gliding the blanket with the child on top of it to one side of the room. Have the child then roll off the blanket onto her or his back. You gently and lovingly cover him or her with the blanket.

You are now free to go to the next child.

NOTE: For additional motor skills with cloth, see *Hello Toes!* on page 17-19.

Burnt Matches

WHAT YOUR CHILDREN WILL GAIN FROM THIS EXPERIENCE		
PHYSICAL/MUSICAL *Balance* *Body Control* *Coordination* *Relaxation* *Eye/Hand Coordination*	*COGNITIVE* *Problem Solving* *Measuring Space* *Visual Memory*	*EMOTIONAL/SOCIAL* *Learning to Be Careful* *Balance* *Relaxation* *Aesthetic Expression*

■ You Need

A minimum of three wooden kitchen matches for each participant. In advance, light and extinguish as many matches as you will use.

A sheet of paper and pencil for each participant.

Bare feet if possible.

■ Finger Balance

CHILDREN   I will give each of you one match.

Sit. Can you figure out how you could balance the match on only one finger? I see that you are doing it! Good!

Here is another match. Balance them both on two different fingers of the same hand. Good!

Here is a third match. Can you balance them on three different fingers?

Good! Change hands.

What movements can you do with your arm or hand without dropping the matches?

■ Arm Balance

CHILDREN   Can you balance all three matches by putting one on the back of your hand, one on your elbow, and one on your shoulder? Now change arms. What movements can you do?

■ Leg Balance

CHILDREN   Can you balance one match on your foot, one on your knee, and one on your thigh? What movements can you make?

Now change legs. Balance the matches. Now move.

■ Wind Games

ADULT   Distribute three matches to each child.

Establish a reasonable goal some distance away for each child to reach using a piece of cardboard or a book or anything else that is convenient. **Be careful to avoid hyperventilation—do not have the children overdo this game.**

CHILDREN   Place only one match on the floor in front of you. I will count to five.

Can you blow five times and get the match to your goal on the count of five? Not before and not after five. One, two, three, four, five.

Good. Let's do it again to see if we can improve. One, two, three, four, five.

This time, place another match in front of you. Can you reach your goal exactly on three? I will count to three: one, two, three.

With your third match, you must try to reach your goal with only one blow! I will count. Ready, set: One!

■ Toe Walk

CHILDREN   All stand. Place your matches between the toes of one bare foot. Now walk.

Give the other foot a turn. Now walk.

■ Balance Walk

CHILDREN   Choose three different places on your body where you can place three matches.

Now walk without letting the matches fall.

Choose three other places. Now choose three others. Remember to use both sides of your body.

■ Match Sculptures

CHILDREN   Place your matches on the floor.

Arrange them in any way that you like to create a beautiful match sculpture. Very good! Can you create another sculpture?

ADULT   Distribute a pencil and a sheet of paper to each child.

CHILDREN   On your paper, draw the sculpture that you created.

Can you create another sculpture and draw that one too?

■ Variations

If you are working with a group of appropriate age, have the children work as partners to draw each other's shapes.

The entire group might draw each child's shape.

You draw a shape on the blackboard. The children create it with their matches.

■ Reconstruction

ADULT　　　　Choose any one of the children's match sculptures.

CHILDREN　　Look carefully at this sculpture. Take one minute to memorize it. Now close your eyes. I am changing the shape just a little bit.

Open your eyes. Can the artist re-create it from the drawing? Let's do another one.

■ Group Sculpture

ADULT　　　　If you are working with only one child, each of you might alternately place one match at a time to build a large sculpture.

CHILDREN　　Sit in a large circle. To start the group sculpture, I am placing a match sculpture that one of you created in the center of the circle.

One at a time, each of you add your three matches to what is already there. Let's take turns around the circle.

You are creating a larger and larger group sculpture.

CHILDREN　　Now one at a time, go to the group sculpture and pick up any three matches without letting anything else move. Is it possible to be careful enough?

Chairs

WHAT YOUR CHILDREN WILL GAIN FROM THIS EXPERIENCE		
PHYSICAL / MUSICAL *Body Control* *Spatial Awareness* *Agility* *Coordination* *Sound & Silence*	COGNITIVE *Problem Solving*	EMOTIONAL / SOCIAL *Confidence* *Fun* *Joy with Others* *Overcoming Fear* *Coping*

■ You Need

Each participant needs a solid chair that will not collapse.

■ Move Around

ADULT   Place each chair in a random pattern with plenty of space around each chair. Be cautious. Prevent the chairs from tipping or falling.

CHILDREN   Keep one hand on your chair. Without lifting your hand, how far in each direction can you walk?

Keep one foot on the chair. How far in each direction can you move?
Solve the same problem with other body parts: your head, your knee, your buttocks, etc.

■ Crawl

CHILDREN   Crawl under the chair.

Without touching the chair's legs, how many different openings can you crawl through?

Crawl through in different ways: backward, on your stomach, on your hands and knees, etc.

How many different ways can you get on and off the chair? Jump? Crawl on and off backward? Through openings?

■ Under & Over

ADULT   Place five or more chairs in a straight line in front of each other (not side by side) so that each chair is touching the back of the chair in front of it.

Hold the hand of any child who needs help.

CHILDREN   Walk between the chairs.
Alternate moving under one chair and onto the next one. How many different ways can you find to move under and over?

Start at one end of the line and step over and onto each chair until you reach the end of the line. Can you do it backward? Be very careful!

Crawl under the line of chairs. Now try it backward.

■ Tunnel

ADULT   The line of chairs is the same as above. Cover the whole line of chairs with a blanket.

CHILDREN   Crawl under the line of chairs. How did that feel?

■ Noncompetitive Musical Chairs

ACCOMPANIMENT
"Sprightly Rhythms"SIDE B, TRACK 5

ADULT   Place the chairs in a straight line, side by side.

An alternate arrangement is to have one chair facing in one direction and the next chair in the opposite direction. The sides of the chairs should touch.

Use as many chairs as you have participants.

42

Use the pause button on your tape recorder to freeze the music. Watch to be sure that all have found a place before resuming the activity.

CHILDREN   When the music plays, move in a circle around the whole line of chairs.

When the music stops, find an empty chair to sit on.

■ Variations

CHILDREN   When the music plays, move around the chairs.

When the music stops, be under a chair. Or, when the music stops, stand behind a chair. Or put one foot on a chair.

NOTE: For additional motor skills with chairs, see *Hello Toes!* on page 13-16.

Elastic

WHAT YOUR CHILDREN WILL GAIN FROM THIS EXPERIENCE		
PHYSICAL / MUSICAL	COGNITIVE	EMOTIONAL / SOCIAL
Body Control	Awareness of Shapes	Imagination
Relaxation	Integration of	Creativity
Balance	Counting, Measuring	Self-Esteem
Centering	& Body Movement	Emotional Centering
Spatial Awareness		Problem Solving

● You Need

A six- to eight-foot piece of elastic for each child. Either tie or sew the ends together, so that it makes a circle.

Bare feet are preferable but not essential.

● Growing Stretch

ADULT   Count slowly and evenly one through ten. Your voice quality will encourage the children to move gradually. The gradual action requires body control and achieves a physical and emotional centering.

CHILDREN   Hold one part of the circle of elastic with two hands in front of you. Stand on the other end with two feet.

Listen to my counting.

As slowly and smoothly as you can, stretch your arms and pull the elastic high over your head.

Try not to reach the top until I reach count ten. One, two, three, four, five, six, seven, eight, nine, ten.

● Shapes

ADULT   Help each child to shape the elastic into a square before continuing. If their feet are as far apart as their hands, they will succeed.

CHILDREN   You are still standing on your elastic.

Can you shape it into a square?

Again, listen to my slow count from one to ten and do your growing stretch: one, two, three, four, five, six, seven, eight, nine, ten.

ADULT   With questions such as "Can you make a round shape?" you will help the children to become aware of the fact that the elastic allows them to make only straight-line shapes.

Do not discourage imitation of other children. They learn from each other.

Help each child to achieve a new shape before continuing.

Alternate each new shape with the growing stretch as you count hypnotically.

CHILDREN   You are still standing on your elastic. Can you make a different shape? A round shape? A triangle?

● Elastic Tunnels

CHILDREN   Each child gets a partner.

Your partner makes a shape with the elastic.

You go through the elastic tunnel.

Now you make a shape with the elastic.

Your partner goes through your elastic tunnel.

Large Scarf

WHAT YOUR CHILDREN WILL GAIN FROM THIS EXPERIENCE		
PHYSICAL / MUSICAL	COGNITIVE	EMOTIONAL / SOCIAL
Eye / Hand & Full-Body Coordination	Conscious Awareness of the Need for Cooperation	Relaxation
Body Response to Musical Phrasing		Group Awareness
Relaxation		Cooperation
		Aesthetics
		Close Adult / Child Connection

NOTE: This magical game can be useful during any of the sessions when you would like the children or child to lie quietly. See Pillow Rest on page 57; Sleep Songs on page 22; the end of Dancing Marionettes on page 8.

ACCOMPANIMENT
"Listening Music" SIDE B, TRACK 2
"Sleep Songs" SIDE A, TRACK 5
"Russian Lullabye" SIDE A, TRACK 2

▲ You Need

A large scarf. You can easily substitute a large bed sheet or a lovely soft bedspread. But this is our favorite: In a fabric store, purchase a three-foot-length of sky-blue translucent material about forty inches wide. Hem both ends to avoid fraying. Its color, texture, and translucent quality evoke responses of wonder and magic.

ADULT

The very first time that you use the large scarf, choose another adult or one of your more confident students to assist you.

▲ Scarf Movement

ADULT &   Each of you holds a corner of the scarf in each hand
ASSISTANT   high over a child who is lying on his or her back.
One of you will stand at the head, the other at the
foot of the child. Step slightly toward each other so
that the scarf is not taut.

Together, lift your arms and flick the scarf upward, to
create a canopy that balloons over the child. The
canopy will keep its shape for a few seconds as you
gently lower your arms.

When the scarf has floated down close to the child,
lift your arms, flick the scarf, and repeat the
movement.

Three or four repetitions of the movement are
sufficient for each child. If you are working with a
group, move quietly from one child to the next.

Listen and move slowly and smoothly with the music.

Dim the lights but do not totally darken the room.

You will find that even the children who are waiting their turn are absorbing the smooth flow and rhythm of the scarf and the music.

▲ Variations

Give each student a chance to be your assistant. Little children will need to hold only one corner of the scarf with two hands. The other corner could be held by an adult or another child.

With practice four children can perform the scarf movement, one on each corner—a beautiful thing to see. They quickly discover that they must coordinate their body movements and work as a team to create the canopy form.

Have a parent lie down next to a child; the scarf movment takes place over the couple.

Pencils

WHAT YOUR CHILDREN WILL GAIN FROM THIS EXPERIENCE		
PHYSICAL / MUSICAL	*COGNITIVE*	*EMOTIONAL / SOCIAL*
Balance / Alignment	*Concentration*	*Cooperation*
Small Muscle Control	*Measuring*	*Aesthetic Expression*
Spatial Awareness	*Awareness of*	*Relaxation*
Relaxation	*Geometric Shapes*	*Balance*

● You Need

Two ordinary—not yet sharpened—full-length pencils for each participant.

Most of these movement games can be done sitting on the floor or at desks. They can also be done standing and using the floor.

● Balance

CHILDREN   Can you balance a pencil, lying crosswise, on one finger? On the other fingers? On your other hand? On your forehead? On your nose? Where else?

● Roll

CHILDREN   With one finger, roll the pencil on the floor or table. Use another finger. Try using your toes.

Can you make it roll by blowing it?

ADULT   Blowing is an excellent activity for creating relaxation. As the breath is released, the muscles relax. **Be careful to avoid hyperventilation.**

● Goal Blow

ADULT   Limit the blowing activity to avoid hyperventilation. Three attempts should be sufficient.

CHILDREN   Place a book or any object that can be used as a goal, a short distance from the pencil.

Blow the pencil until it hits the goal.

Make the distance to the goal longer and longer.

● Push

CHILDREN   With your thumb, push the pencil, lying lengthwise, forward, sideways, to the other side, backward. What other part of your body can you push with?

● Two-Pencil Push

ADULT   Place two pencils parallel and lengthwise on the floor in front yourself and each child. Demonstrate as you instruct.

CHILDREN   Your two pencils are parallel. What do you think I
            mean by "parallel"?

            With your two thumbs, can you move the two pencils
            forward and still kepp them parallel? Backward? Any
            other direction?

● Designs

CHILDREN   Create a design with your two pencils—on the floor.
            Now try to make a design in the air. Create another
            one. And another.

● Jumping

ADULT   Put enough space between two parallel pencils so
            that there is enough room for the children to jump
            between the two pencils.

CHILDREN   Jump between the two pencils.

            And jump out again.

            Each time that you jump push the pencils apart,
            making more space between the pencils.

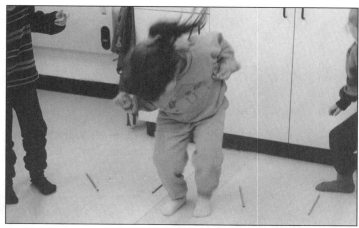

Jump between the two pencils. And jump out again. It doesn't matter whether you jump with both feet or one foot at a time.

Keep making more space between the pencils.

● Triangular Shapes

ADULT   The next two games are for a full class or group.

CHILDREN   One at a time, place your pencil on the floor.

Each child adds another pencil to help create a triangular shape on the floor.

How many triangles can you make?

● Square Shapes

CHILDREN   Now each of you can help to create a square shape.

Each child places another pencil on the floor to help create a square. Is it possible to make round shapes with pencils?

Pillow

WHAT YOUR CHILDREN WILL GAIN FROM THIS EXPERIENCE		
PHYSICAL / MUSICAL Spatial Awareness Leg Stretches Body Stretches Coordination Relaxation	COGNITIVE Problem Solving	EMOTIONAL / SOCIAL Relaxation Fun

▲ You Need

A large pillow for each child. The pillow needs to be large enough so that you will be able to pull it for the Pillow Slide without too much difficulty.

▲ Pillow Rock

ACCOMPANIMENT
"Russian Lullabye" SIDE A, TRACK 2
"Goodnight Song" SIDE A, TRACK 4
"Sleep Songs" SIDE A, TRACK 5

CHILDREN   Sit on the center of your pillow.

Hold each end of the pillow.

Rock from side to side, rocking the pillow with you.

▲ Pillow Sleep

CHILDREN   Lie on your back with only your head on the pillow. Your head is fast asleep.

Lie on your back with only your hand on the pillow. Your hand is fast asleep.

Lie on your back with only your foot on the pillow. Your foot is fast asleep.

ADULT Continue this game by naming various other body parts. However, avoid continuing if you see signs of overstimulation.

End the pillow sleep with a repetition of the head on the pillow and a slow count on your part from one to ten.

▲ Pillow Pass

CHILDREN Sit on the floor. Pass the pillow under your knees from one side to the other side four times.

Sit with the pillow in front of you. Pass the pillow backward under your buttocks.

Now pass the pillow forward under your buttocks.

Go fackward and forward four times.

▲ Pillow Walk

CHILDREN   Walk forward and backward on top of the pillow.

▲ Pillow Stretch

CHILDREN   Stand with your legs apart. The pillow is in front of you on the floor. You cannot move your feet.

With your hands in front of you, bend over to touch the pillow. Feel the stretch in your legs.

Staying in the same place, push the pillow forward with your hands so it is slightly father away from you.

Place both hands on the pillow and feel the stretch in your legs and in your back.

Once more, push the pillow forward and then again and again until you are lying on your stomach with the pillow way in front of your fingers!

Stretch your arms as far forward as you can and stretch your legs as far behind you as you can.

▲ Pillow Rest

ACCOMPANIMENT
"Goodnight Song" SIDE A, TRACK 4
"Sleep Songs" SIDE A, TRACK 5

CHILDREN   Stay on your stomach. Put your head on the pillow. Relax. Now I will put the music on. Go to sleep.

ADULT   Only at this point do you add the music.

▲ Pillow Slide

ACCOMPANIMENT
"Hit the Road to Dreamland" SIDE A, TRACK 6

ADULT   Approach one child at a time and help the child to place the pillow under his or her stomach.

Grasp the pillow and gently drag the pillow and child to one side of the room.

Each child gets a turn.

Plastic Bottles

WHAT YOUR CHILDREN WILL GAIN FROM THIS EXPERIENCE		

PHYSICAL / MUSICAL
Body Control
Spatial Awareness
Control of Small
   Muscles
	COGNITIVE
	Awareness of Physical
	   Elements; Air waves;
	   Gravity; Weight;
	   Density; Shape
	Language
		EMOTIONAL / SOCIAL
		Stress Management
		Concentration
		Focus
		Attentiveness
		Self-Discipline
		Fun
		Learning to Be Careful

■ You Need

One large empty plastic bottle for each participant and a smooth floor.

A small or medium-sized ball. The younger the children are, the larger the ball must be.

■ Bottle Touch

CHILDREN
You are sitting or standing next to your upright bottle.

Can you touch the top of the bottle with your finger so lightly that it does not fall—or even move?

Can you carefully touch it with the palm of your hand? Your elbow? Your shoulder? Your chin? Your forehead? Your knee? Your toes?

Which part makes it fall? Why?

ADULT
Help the children to understand a fast movement can create air waves that can make the bottle fall even if it is not touched. Talk about other physical elements: gravity (would it matter if we turned this bottle upside down?); weight (would it make a difference if we

used a heavy glass bottle?); density (will the bottle fall if we fill it with water?); shape (would it make a difference if we used a much shorter bottle?)—when it is appropriate.

There need be no feeling of failure on any child's part. We cannot expect a three-year-old to touch the bottle with a knee without a quiver. But a five-year-old can probably do it. Set an atmosphere of experimentation: "Let's find out which parts can touch the bottle without moving it." When safety is established, the pleasure comes from the trying.

■ Obstacle Course

ADULT   Place five or more upright bottles in a random pattern around the room.

CHILDREN   One at a time, move between and around the bottles without touching them.

             Did some fall down? Why do you think that happened? Let's try it again.

■ Rolling Bottle

ADULT   Always encourage the use of both sides of the body.

CHILDREN   Lay your bottle flat on the floor. Place your hand on the bottle and press gently.

             Roll the bottle back and forth.

             Now use the other hand.

             Can you make it roll with your foot?

             Now use the other foot.

             What other part of the body can make the bottle roll? Your elbow? Your knee? Your head? Your nose?

■ Bowling Bottles

CHILDREN   Stand away from the bottles. Roll a ball
            toward the bottles.

            How many did you make fall?

            How many are still standing? Try again.

Pole Sway

WHAT YOUR CHILDREN WILL GAIN FROM THIS EXPERIENCE		
PHYSICAL / MUSICAL	COGNITIVE	EMOTIONAL / SOCIAL
Kinesthetic Awareness of Own Body Rhythm Awareness of Group Rhythm Integrating Voice and Body Movement	Conscious Awareness of the Need for Cooperation	Stress Management Belonging to the Group Self-Esteem

ACCOMPANIMENT
"Goodnight Song" SIDE A, TRACK 4

● You Need

A pole that is preferably eight feet long. If you have only a shorter broomstick, it will do.

ADULT

Hold one end of the pole. An assistant or student holds the other end.

Both you and your assistant stand with one foot back, so that you can comfortably sway with the pole. The pole is moving toward one of you and then toward the other. For the moment, the class is observing only.

Ask three to five children (depending on the size of the pole) to stand in a line, with both hands touching the pole. They are facing the class.

Lift the pole to the height of the children's chests.

It is necessary to start the entire activity in silence, so that the children become kinesthetically aware of their own body rhythms and the rhythm of the group. You may choose to start the music when the entire

class has joined the activity, or you may choose to
teach musical phrasing, by having each new line join
at the beginning of a new phrase.

At any point, ask the class to sing along with the
music.

CHILDREN	Touch the pole softly. Your fingers are like feathers.
	Separate your feet slightly, so that when you feel the pole move from side to side, you can bend one knee and then the other to move with the movement of the pole.
ADULT	Be careful to keep the rhythm slow enough so that it gradually becomes mesmerizing. Be sure that each child has become involved before progressing to the next step.
	The child closest to you puts her or his hand on your shoulder.
CHILDREN	Lift the hand that is closest to me. Put it onto the shoulder of the person next to you. Continue to sway.
	If you like, you may close your eyes and feel yourself swaying with both the pole and the whole line of children. Continue to sway. Take the other hand off the pole and just let it relax and drop by your side.
ADULT	At this point you may remove the pole. Ask the assistant to lower it quietly to the floor.
	Ask more children to stand behind the swaying group. They join the rhythm and the movement by putting one hand on a shoulder of a person in front of them.

Rope

WHAT YOUR CHILDREN WILL GAIN FROM THIS EXPERIENCE		

PHYSICAL / MUSICAL
Coordination
Body Control
Tactile Sense
Spatial Awareness
	COGNITIVE
	Measuring
	Geometric Concepts
	Integrating Cognition
	   with Movement
	   Activity
		EMOTIONAL / SOCIAL
		Imagination
		Relaxation
		Fun

▲ You Need

A four- or five-foot-long pliable cotton rope for each participant. (Nylon ropes tend to be too stiff.)

▲ Big & Small

CHILDREN   With your feet only, make a rope as small as you can.

With your feet, stretch the rope to make it as long as possible.

With your hands, make the rope small, then long.

With your eyes closed and using your hands, make the rope small, then long, then small, then long again.

▲ Rolling Rope

ADULT   Help the children to center themselves with the rope stretched horizontally in front of them.

CHILDREN   Sit on the floor. The rope is lying in front of you.

Stretch it out with both hands.

Sit yourself exactly by the middle of the rope.

With your hands, roll the rope forward and backward. Watch the ends of the rope—what happened to the ends?

Roll the rope forward and backward with your feet.

ADULT　　　The stretching activities that are done with a towel on pages 94-98 can also be done with rope.

▲ Rope Walk

CHILDREN　　Choose one end of the rope and walk on it to the other end backward.

Can you go forward and backward with your eyes closed?

With your eyes open, go forward to the middle and backward. Turn around, now go backward to the middle and forward again.

▲ Rope Street

ADULT　　　On the floor, place a series of ropes end to end to form an imaginary street. The street can curve for added interest.

CHILDREN　　Walk or crawl forward and backward on this imaginary street.

▲ Imaginary Ropes

CHILDREN　　We just imagined that the ropes were a street and we walked on the street. With your own rope each of you think about what else the rope could be. Don't tell us—do something with the rope to show us what you are imagining.

ADULT　　　You may need to give an example—a snake; a hole in the ground—to help them along. Have the class guess what the rope is after each child's performance.

Then you guess before asking the child what it was.

The variety of movements created by the children can lead to additional activities, e.g., leaping over an imaginary stream.

▲ Circle Rope

CHILDREN Make a circle on the floor with your rope.

Stand in the middle of the rope circle. How do you know that you are in the middle?

Stand outside of the rope circle.

Put one hand in the center, now the other hand.

Put one foot in the center, now the other foot.

What other body part can you put into the center?

▲ Round House

CHILDREN Stand in the center of your circle rope.

Pretend that it is a round house and this is where you live.

You are the smallest person in the world, as small as a mouse.

Open a tiny window and peek out.

Anybody there? No answer.

Put your whole head out. Hello there! No answer.

Open a tiny door and squeeze yourself out of the door.

How can you get out of such a tiny door?

You are out! Walk around, or crawl all around your orund house to see if anyone is watching you. No one's around.

Squeeze back into your round house.

Curl yourself up inside and go to sleep.

Scarves

WHAT YOUR CHILDREN WILL GAIN FROM THIS EXPERIENCE		
PHYSICAL / MUSICAL *Full Body Stretch* *Laterality* *Musicality* *Awareness of Tempo* *Body Control* *Relaxation*	COGNITIVE *Aid to Reading* *Awareness of Colors*	EMOTIONAL / SOCIAL *Imagination* *Relaxation* *Expression of Love*

■ You Need

At least one soft translucent scarf for each participant; for some activities two scarves per person will be needed. If possible, find scarves that will float, rather than fall, when you throw them into the air. The smaller and thinner the scarf, the more easily it floats.

■ Naughty Puppy

ACCOMPANIMENT
"Rhythm Game" SIDE B, TRACK 6

ADULT

As you become familiar with the accompanying music, you will time your telling of the story—dragging out the last words—to coincide with the sudden changes in the music.

To prevent the scarves from flying in the air—and to keep the children from becoming too excited—tell them the puppy's feet must stay on the ground. Puppies cannot run in the air.

You need not be concerned about excitement. The immediate change to the slow music disciplines the children and structures the inner quiet. Stop the game whenever you like, always ending with the slow, quiet music.

CHILDREN The scarf is your puppy. Take it out for a walk. Watch it walking a little behind you, on the ground.

Today your puppy is behaving very well.

Walk backward and look at puppy in front of you.

You are really surprised, because usually when you take puppy out for a walk—oh, oh! You are pulling me around and around!

I'm holding onto you and making you stay on the ground.

I'm going around and around. What a naughty puppy!

Now I'm going the other way.

Suddenly you change your mind—you want to walk slowly again. What a sweet puppy you are.

Oh, oh! The puppy is so tired. Let it rest on the floor.

Put your head on the soft puppy and you rest, too.

■ Balance & Walk

ACCOMPANIMENT
"Listening Music" SIDE B, TRACK 2

CHILDREN Place your scarf over one hand. Walk slowly and carefully to keep the scarf in place. Now walk backward.

Turn slowly, then turn the other way.

Place the scarf on your elbow. On the other elbow. On your shoulder. On the other shoulder. On your palm.

Balance the scarf on your palm as you slowly sit and slowly stand.

How else can you balance the scarf?

■ Double Dancing Scarves

ACCOMPANIMENT
"Listening Music" SIDE B, TRACK 2

ADULT Demonstrate this activity for a class. Ask one child to be your partner.

Have the child hold the corners of two scarves—one in each hand.

Face the child and take the opposite corners of the scarves in each of your hands.

The scarves are now parallel to each other.

Watch your partner's hands intently, so that both scarves move slowly and smoothly together. Move the scarves from side to side, then toward each other and apart, high and low, all around.

CHILDREN   Watch to see how careful we are. We do not pull or
            stretch the scarves, because they are delicate and
            can tear. We move them gently and smoothly.
            Now it's your turn. You try with a partner.

■ Flying Scarf

ADULT   Demonstrate the movement so that the children can
            see your scarf flying through space before attempting
            it themselves.

            Young children need to be encouraged to stretch from
            toes to fingertips. They prefer to curl up and retain the
            comfortable, secure position that their bodies recall
            from the womb.
            Each child will need your help individually to hold the
            scarf properly.

            Stand behind the child whose hands are high and
            holding two corners of the the scarf. Take the other
            two corners of the scarf in your two hands. Stretch it
            toward you (behind the child) like a flat ceiling.

            As you say "run," let go of the scarf and watch it fly
            freely through space above the running child.

CHILDREN   Hold two corners of your scarf.

            Put your hands up over your head as high as you
            can, and when I say so, run. Look up at the scarf,
            stretch your arms, and run.

■ Balance & Float

            ACCOMPANIMENT
            "Goodnight Song" SIDE A, TRACK 4
            "Greensleeves" SIDE B, TRACK 7

CHILDREN   Place your scarf over your hand and swing your arm
            from side to side. Your scarf is dancing and floating.

Place the scarf on your other hand. Make it float and dance.

Now sit down. Place the scarf over your foot. Put your hands on the floor, lift your scarf-covered leg, and make your leg dance. Now place the scarf on the other leg. Make that scarf-covered leg dance.

■ The Other Hand

ADULT The major purpose of this activity is to encourage the use of the "other," less dominant, hand. Constantly finding new ways to motivate the children to use both sides of their bodies can facilitate their reading abilities.

CHILDREN Sit with your scarf in one hand. Keep the scarf soft and loose. Do not squeeze it into a ball.

Toss the scarf up in the air and catch it with your other hand.

Toss it up again with that hand and catch it with the first hand. Keep changing from one hand to the other—toss and catch and toss and catch.

■ Variation

This activitity can also be done standing up.

■ Mirror Toss

CHILD Only one scarf is needed for this activity. Find a partner, then sit, facing your sitting partner, and hold your scarf in one hand. Toss it to your partner.

PARTNER Catch the scarf with the hand that is on the same side as your partner's tossing arm—like a mirror reflection.

With the same hand, toss the scarf back to your partner.

CHILD   Using the same hand, toss back and forth until it
                 becomes easy and smooth.

                 Then change to your other hand.

■ Variation

This activitity can also be done standing up.

■ The Square Circle

CHILDREN   Find a partner, then sit, facing your sitting partner.
                 Can you toss and catch the scarf making a square
                 circle? Toss the scarf from one hand to your other
                 hand. Then toss to your partner's hand who will toss
                 the scarf to his or her other hand. Then catch the
                 scarf and toss to your other hand.

                 Around and around, making a square circle! Now
                 go the other way around.

■ Variation

This activitity can also be done standing up.

■ Group Circle

ADULT   Have the children sit in a circle facing the center.

                 The first child tosses the scarf to his or her "other"
                 hand, then to the next person in the circle. In that
                 way, the scarf travels around the circle.

                 After each hand of each child is activated, reverse
                 the circle.

■ Variation

This activitity can also be done standing up.

74

■ Weeping Willow Tree

ADULT   Each participant will need two scarves. The major goal is to give children's upper torsos the longest possible stretch. Encourage the children to continue facing forward for the best results. When the exercise is done correctly, two to four stretches are adequate.

CHILDREN   Stand with your feet slightly apart.

Stand very firmly because your legs are the roots of a tree deep, deep in the ground.

Your body is the trunk of the tree. Your arms are the branches. The scarves are the leaves.

Reach your arms very high overhead.

You are a tall weeping willow tree.

Bend way over to one side, then grow straight and tall again.

Bend way over to the other side, now grow straight and tall once more.

■ Group Magic Mirror Scarves

ACCOMPANIMENT
"Sleep Songs" SIDE A, TRACK 5
"Russian Lullabye" SIDEA A, TRACK 2
"Goodnight Song" SIDE A, TRACK 4

ADULT   Each participant holds one scarf at its corner. You stand facing the group, holding your scarf in your left hand while the children hold their scarves in their right hands—they will be a mirror reflection of you. Move very, very slowly, letting your eyes focus intently first on one child's scarf, then on another's. Feel a magnetism between your arm and the children's taking place as if your arm could really control the timing of the child's arm.

Play the music very quietly and move your arm slowly as you talk to the children.

Do very simple movements—even for the older children. The important thing is not how creative or how beautifully you can move but how connected you and the children can become. Trust will inevitably follow.

CHILDREN   Our scarves are magic.

If we are very quiet, your scarf can hear my scarf saying, "Move with me. I like you. I want to be your friend."

We can even imagine that we are holding another scarf in the other hand. They also can hear each other.

■ Pillow Scarf

ACCOMPANIMENT
"Sleep Songs" SIDE A, TRACK 5
"Russian Lullabye" SIDEA A, TRACK 2
"Goodnight Song" SIDE A, TRACK 4

CHILDREN   Fold your scarf carefully into the shape of a pillow. Place it on the floor.

Put your head on the pillow.

Listen to the music and rest.

■ Colors

ADULT   This is a good follow-up to the above game. Allow those children who can to rest longer while you speak quietly to those children ready to move again. Call the children according to the color of their scarves to come to you one at a time and direct them to where their shoes are waiting.

In the meantime, the other children are resting.

CHILDREN   If your scarf is red, stand slowly and bring your scarf to me.

If your scarf is yellow, stand slowly and bring your scarf to me.

If your scarf is green, etc.

Sponges

WHAT YOUR CHILDREN WILL GAIN FROM THIS EXPERIENCE		
PHYSICAL / MUSICAL Full Body Stretch Laterality Awareness Rhythm Body Control Tactile	COGNITIVE Cause & Effect Power of Air Waves Awareness of Textures	EMOTIONAL / SOCIAL Confidence Fun Stamina

● You Need

Two to five ordinary rectangular household sponges for each participant. A variety of colored sponges is fun.

● Tapping Rhythm

ACCOMPANIMENT
"Sprightly Rhythms" SIDE B, TRACK 5

ADULT   Each child has a sponge. Have the children sit on the floor. Simply put the music on and sit down with your own sponge. Speak each verse rhythmically two times and then proceed to other body parts. Encourage the children to imitate you.

CHILDREN   Tap the sponge
On your head
To the beat
Of the music.

Tap the sponge
On your head
To the beat
Of the music.

ADULT   Other body parts on which to tap the sponge:
               shoulder; other shoulder; knee; other knee; on each
               knee (alternate knees); toes; other toes; elbow; other
               elbow (sponge in opposite hand); back (sponge in
               one hand, then the other); buttocks (sponge in one
               hand, then the other).

               Encourage the children to change (where indicated)
               from their dominant arm to the weaker one. The
               weaker arm will become stronger and more
               confident.

               Please participate, whether working with a single
               child or a group.

               Smile and have fun while rhythmically repeating the
               name of the body part.

               Change to a new body part when you see that all of
               the children are with you.

● Sponge Stretch

ADULT   Stand in front of a child. Hold a sponge in each
               hand.

               Lift the sponges high enough so that the child must
               reach and stretch (and possibly jump if old enough)
               to touch each sponge. The child under three years of
               age may not yet be ready to jump.

               Adjust the height of the sponges for each child to be
               sure that each succeeds in touuching the sponges.

               Young children need to be encouraged to stretch from
               toes to fingertips. They tend to prefer to curl up and
               retain the comfortable, secure position that their
               bodies remember from the womb.

CHILDREN   Stretch and touch one sponge with one hand. Now
               touch the other sponge with your other hand. Now
               touch both sponges at the same time with both hands.

               One hand, the other hand, both hands!

80

● Rolling Logs

ADULT   Place four or five sponges on the floor in a straight row. They represent small rocks in a stream.

CHILDREN   The sponges are rocks. They are lying in a stream.

The water in stream is rolling over the rocks.

Do you think that it hurts the water to roll over the rocks?

Let's find out. You be the water.

One at a time, lie down and slowly, very slowly, roll over each sponge until you get to the other side of the row.

Did that hurt? Can you guess why not?

● Merry-Go-Round

CHILDREN   Sit on the floor. Hold the sponge between your feet. Put your hands on the floor. Pick up the sponge with your feet.

Still sitting on the floor, push yourself with your hands around and around.

Now go the other way.

● Flying Sponge

CHILDREN   Sit with a sponge between your feets

When I count to "three," send the sponge flying straight up into the air and try to catch it with your hands.

One, two, three!

Put the sponge back between your feet again and try to send it up so that you will be able to catch it. Practice.

● Sponge Balance

ADULT   Activate as many body parts as possible.

Keep your voice soft and quiet as though not wanting to disturb the sponge.

Encourage the use of the "other" hand and foot to activate the weaker side.

Repeat the use of the body parts that seem to need additional practice.

CHILDREN   Sit on the floor. Stand your sponge upright on the floor. Will it fall if you are not careful?

Try to touch it with one finger so carefully that it does not fall.

Now touch the sponge with one finger of your other hand.

What else can you touch the sponge with but keep it from falling?

● Skyscraper

ADULT   Have each child sit on the floor with two sponges.

CHILDREN   Sit on the floor with one sponge balanced on its end in front of you. Be careful not to let it fall.

Now place a second sponge balanced, also on its end, on top of the first one.

Watch them balancing. Can you blow only the top sponge off?

Now blow the bottom sponge over.

What makes the sponge fall? You did, yes. And what did you blow out of your mouth? Your breath, your air.

ADULT   You want to have children become aware that it's the movement of their breath—air waves—that caused the fall. Other examples and further discussion can take place with the older children.

● Sponge Walk

ADULT   Place the sponges upright in a random pattern around the room. Leave plenty of space between the sponges for the children to walk between and around them.

If you think your group can handle it, place a second sponge on top of the first—as in Skyscraper, the above game.

CHILDREN   One or two at a time, walk around and between the sponges. Be careful. Keep them from falling. If one falls, I will fix it.

ADULT   After the experience, sit and talk with the children. Ask what made the sponge(s) fall. Discuss what the children each did to keep the sponge(s) from falling.

Bring them to the realization that if touched even slightly—even if they get just a little too close—the sponge(s) might fall. The children learn that even the slightest movement of their bodies creates an air wave.

● Variation

If you think that the children can handle it, try having them run instead of walk. Then discuss the differences that different tempos can make in air waves.

● Sponge Sculpture

CHILDREN   One at a time, each of you place your sponge on the floor in front of me.

The sponge can be upright or flat or on its side—you decide. You can also decide whether you want your sponge to touch another sponge or not.

You are creating a group sculpture.

ADULT   When the group sculpture has been completed, ask the children to tell you what each thinks it represents or look like.

It might be of special interest to the children for you to notice and characterize the children's placement of the sponge. Does the sponge want to become part of the group? Does it want to be alone?

CHILDREN   As I say your name, lift one sponge off of the sculpture without toppling the design and hand it to me. Then walk quietly to your shoes (or out the door).

NOTE: For additional movement games with sponges, see *Hello Toes!* on pages 60-68.

Superball™

<table>
<tr><td colspan="3" align="center">WHAT YOUR CHILDREN WILL GAIN FROM THIS
EXPERIENCE</td></tr>
<tr><td>PHYSICAL / MUSICAL
Body Control
Articulation of Body
   Parts
Tactile Awareness
Coordination</td><td>COGNITIVE
Measuring Space;
   Time; Energy Levels
Coordinating Right
   and Left
Hemispheres of the
   Brain.</td><td>EMOTIONAL / SOCIAL
Patience
Observation
Concentration
Self-Discipline</td></tr>
</table>

▲ You Need

A Superball™ for each participant. Superball™ is the trade name for a small ball that has the capacity to bounce extremely high.

Bare feet are preferable.

▲ Press

CHILDREN   Sit on the floor. The Superball™ is on the floor in front of you.

Press down hard on the ball with each finger. Now try one hand, now the other hand.

Press down with your toes. Now try one foot, now the other foot.

What other body parts can you press hard? Your elbow? Your other elbow? Your head? What else? Always remember if you one side, use the other side.

▲ Pick Up

CHILDREN   Stand. Pick up the ball with only your toes. Now use your other foot.

▲ Throw

CHILDREN   Everybody, stand with your backs to one wall. At my signal, throw your ball to the opposite wall and wait. Watch to see where it finally lands. When you are sure that all of the balls have stopped rolling, raise your hand.

▲ Roll

ADULT   The line of children should be close enough to the wall for even the youngest child to have some success.

CHILDREN   Together, let's choose a wall to be our goal.

Everyone, sit in a line facing the goal wall, each the same distance from it.

At my signal, roll the ball toward the goal wall.

Go!

Did your ball hit the wall and bounce back to you?

Do you know why?

Did you use too much energy? Not enough?

Did you throw instead of roll?

Do you think that if you practice, your body will get to know just how much energy you need to get the ball as close to the wall as possible?

Try again.

▲ Design

CHILDREN   One at a time, come to the center of the room and place your ball on the floor.

Your ball must not touch any other ball.

What does the design look like to you?

Do you like it? Why? No? Why not?

Let's make another design.

Tennis Balls

WHAT YOUR CHILDREN WILL GAIN FROM THIS EXPERIENCE		
PHYSICAL / MUSICAL	COGNITIVE	EMOTIONAL / SOCIAL

Balance
Muscle Toning
Articulation of Body
    Parts
Relaxation
Feeling a Musical
    Phrase
Body Control
Stretches
Coordinating Body with
    the Music
	Naming Body Parts
	Concentration
	Problem Solving
	Awareness of Weight
		Learning to be Careful
		Joy of Moving to Music
		Partner Games

■ You Need

A ball for each participant. Old, used tennis balls that no longer bounce are excellent.

Bare feet are best whenever possible.

■ Heel Press

CHILDREN   Stand up. The tennis ball is on the floor next to you. Place the ball under your heel, while keeping your toes on the floor.

Press down and squeeze the ball with your heel.

Release and press down and sqeeze five times.

Can you feel the exercise your heel is getting? Now try with your other heel.

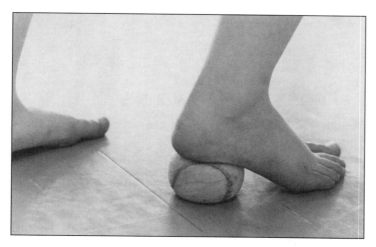

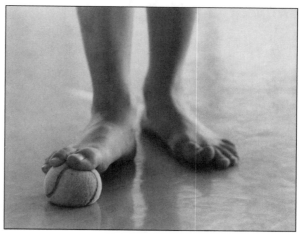

■ Toes Press

CHILDREN   Place the ball under the toes of one foot. Keep your heel on the floor.

Press down and squeeze the ball with all of your toes.

Can you feel your big toe pressing? Your little toe?

Change feet and press with the toes on your other foot.

■ Foot Press

CHILDREN   Your toes are pressing down on the ball.

Glide your foot forward—still pressing down. Feel the ball roll to your heel. Keep pressing and roll it back again to your toes. Go back and forth.

Can you feel the exercise that your foot is getting?

■ Hand Press

ADULT   Because the children send their weight forward in this wide position, they get a stretch in their legs, backs, and hands.

CHILDREN   Your ball is on the floor in front of you.

Stand with your feet apart, toes pointed out.

Bend both knees away from each other. Place one hand flat on the floor with all of the fingers stretched. Place the palm of the other hand on the ball.

Press and roll the ball from your fingers to the heel of your hand, as you did with your foot. Press it back and forth. Now use your other hand to press and roll. Can you feel the exercise that your hand is getting? Can you touch your head to the ball in the same position?

■ Balance

ACCOMPANIMENT
"Listening Music" SIDE B, TRACK 2

CHILDREN   Stand and place the ball on your open palm. Slowly walk forward listening to the music. Try to keep the ball from dropping. Can you carefully walk backward?

Where else can you balance the ball?

Can you sit and balance? Where? Can you lie down?

■ Ball Toss

ACCOMPANIMENT
"Goodnight Song" SIDE A, TRACK 4

CHILDREN   Sit. Move with the music. Toss the ball from one hand to the other to the rhythm of the music.

Open both arms wide, then lift them high overhead. Look up at the ball as you put it into the other hand.

Bring both arms down and repeat the movement, making your ball and arms dance with the music.

Change hands. Feel the weight of the ball.

ADULT   For older children, the space between the hands can gradually become larger and larger. They can also be encouraged to sway from side to side in their torso, coordinating their body movement with the movement of the ball.

■ Thigh Pass

ACCOMPANIMENT
"Goodnight Song" SIDE A, TRACK 4

CHILDREN   Sit on the floor. Lift one leg and pass the ball under your thigh to the other hand.

Lift both arms overhead, as you did in Ball Toss, the activity above. Move with the music.

Change legs. Can you pass the ball under both thighs?

ADULT   The older children can be encouraged to keep their feet off the floor. The young ones will probably keep them down.

The high lift of the arms and the torso between the pass, in addition to giving a lovely feeling in the body, will give the children an opportunity to stretch and lengthen their backs.

The older children can also be encouraged to lift both the buttock and the leg off the floor, so that they must momentarily balance on one buttock.

■ Overhand Pass

ACCOMPANIMENT
"Goodnight Song" SIDE A, TRACK 4

CHILDREN   Sit or stand.

Lift the ball overhead and let it drop gently into the other hand. Feel the ball dancing and move with the music.

Can you move through space as you pass the ball? With a partner? How else?

■ Feet Toss

CHILDREN   Sit on the floor. Place the ball between both feet. Your knees are bent, your feet are holding the ball firmly.

Place your hands on the floor behind you to hold your balance.

With your feet, toss the ball into the air and catch it with your hands. It will take practice to catch it before it drops to the floor. Can you do it with a partner? The partner can catch the ball with his or her hands, then toss it back with his or her feet.

■ Inching the Ball

CHILDREN   Everybody get on your hands and knees. The ball is in front of you.

Keeping your hands on the floor, touch the ball with only your forehead and move it forward. Do not press—just touch it lightly and inch it along the floor.

Can you inch the ball with your nose? Your elbow? Your other elbow? Your knee? Your other knee?

Can you inch the ball backward with your knee?

■ Cat Stretch

CHILDREN You are on your hands and knees.

Place the ball under one hand.

Press and squeeze and roll the ball from your fingers to your wrist to your forearm to your elbow. Stay low with your body.

Keep pressing and roll it back again.

Can you feel the ball massaging your arm?

Can you feel your back stretching like a cat's?

Give the other arm a turn.

Towel

WHAT YOUR CHILDREN WILL GAIN FROM THIS EXPERIENCE		
PHYSICAL / MUSICAL Full Body Stretches Body Control Balance Relaxation Coordination	COGNITIVE Measuring Time Awareness of Time & Space Problem Solving	EMOTIONAL / SOCIAL Relaxation Balance

● You Need

A towel for each participant. For the older children, a bath towel presents a greater challenge.

Bare feet or socks are preferable.

● Time Control

CHILDREN

Sit on the floor in any comfortable position.

Roll the towel lengthwise, making it as long as possible.

Stretch the rolled towel out horizontally in front of you.

Place both hands on the towel's exact center.

Now smoothly, slowly, glide each hand to each end of the towel. Reach both ends at the same time.

Can you also do it with your eyes closed? Can you use your feet? Your elbows?

Now sit on your knees. Place your chin on the towel. Slide your hands outward to each end of the towel.

Try to reach both ends at the same time.

Can you feel the stretch? Where?

● Cross Stretch

CHILDREN   Sit on your knees. Place the rolled towel horizontally in front of you. Cross your arms in front of your body.

Reach one hand to touch the opposite end of the towel. Keep it there.

Stretch with the other hand and try to reach across your arm to touch the other end.

Can you feel the stretch? Where?

Change hands and give the other arm a turn.

● Leg Cross Stretch

CHILDREN   Lie on your back with your head on or near the center of the rolled towel. Your arms are open, touching the floor.

Lift one leg and cross it over the other leg. Try to touch the end of the towel with your lifted leg.

Give the other leg a turn. Can you feel the stretch? Where?

Now, still on your back, place your feet on the center of the rolled towel.

Your arms are by your sides touching the floor. Keep them there.

Lift one leg and cross it over the other leg. Touch the end of the towel with your lifted leg.

Give the other leg a turn.

Can you feel the stretch? Where?

● Open Door

CHILDREN   Lie on your back. Place your head on or near the center of the rolled towel.

Place both hands on your stomach. Lift both legs.

Open them wide apart. Point your feet toward each of the ends of the towel.

Hold that position for a few seconds.

Can you feel the stretch? Where?

● Towel Push Stretch

CHILDREN   Sit on the floor. Hold the rolled towel in your hands on each end.

Place one foot on the center of the towel. With your foot, push the towel away from you while you hold it tightly with both hands. The towel will lift slightly off the floor.

Let the pushing leg bend at the knee, and then push and stretch. Again, bend and stretch.

Can you feel the stretch? Where?

● Over the Hurdle

CHILDREN   Stand. Hold the rolled towel in front of you, each hand holding an end.

Lower your arms and step over the towel. Hold it firmly. Step first with one foot and then the other. Now go backward and forward and backward again.

Give the other leg a chance to lead.

● Drying Yourself

ACCOMPANIMENT
"Sprightly Rhythms" SIDE B, TRACK 5

CHILDREN   Stand. Hold the towel on both ends.

Lift the towel over your head to the back of your neck. Imagine that you have just come out of the bath.

Dry yourself with the towel by sliding it from side to

side. Stretch one arm and then the other. Be sure that your neck is dry.

Now dry your shoulders.

How else can you dry yourself? Dry a partner.

● Towel Dance

ACCOMPANIMENT
"Listening Music" SIDE B, TRACK 2
"Sprightly Rhythms" SIDE B, TRACK 5

ADULT If you are working with a group, use this opportunity to allow them to perform for each other. If you would like to add music, choose any of our selections.

CHILDREN The towel is on the floor. Unroll it and make it flat and smooth. Stand on it.

      If you were not allowed to touch the floor around your towel with any part of your body, what kind of movements could you do in such a small space?

● Hammock

ACCOMPANIMENT
"Goodnight Song" SIDE A, TRACK 4
"Russian Lullabye" SIDE A, TRACK 2

ADULT This can only be done if you have two strong adults to hold the "hammock" firmly and safely.

      Place the towel flat on the floor. Place one child face up and lengthwise, parallel to the length of the towel. Pick up one end in each hand, so that all four ends will come up together. Be sure to get a firm grip.

      Lift the towel with the child very slightly off the floor. Listen to the slow rhythms of the music and gently rock the "hammock" from side to side.

ADULT   Smile at the child as you rock. Hum with the music.
               Feel the rhythm in your own body.

● Pillow Rest

> *ACCOMPANIMENT*
> *"Sleep Songs" SIDE A, TRACK 5*

CHILDREN   Fold your towel as many times as needed to make a
               pillow.

               Place your head on the pillow, listen to the music,
               and rest.

PART THREE:
Movement Games
Using Your Imagination

Magic Balloons

WHAT YOUR CHILDREN WILL GAIN FROM THIS EXPERIENCE		
PHYSICAL / MUSICAL *Body Control* *Body Centering*	COGNITIVE *Problem Solving* *Awareness of Shapes &* *Sizes*	EMOTIONAL / SOCIAL *Self-Discipline* *Confidence* *Self-Esteem* *Imagination* *Joy*

▲ Magic Balloons

ADULT

Your goal is to have all of the children standing in their final balloon shapes after about five blows. Ask them to freeze their shapes for a few seconds after each blow. They are learning to control the needed muscles and joints.

You will find that Magic Balloons can be used anytime you notice a child standing or moving with hunched shoulders or any of the other ways in which our bodies carry our tensions.

You may also introduce this game with The Magic Basket story on page 18.

CHILDREN

Let's make magic and turn you into balloons. Each of you tell me what color you would like to be.

Lie flat on the floor. You have no air. You know, balloons come in different shapes. So when I blow a little bit of air into your balloon, you grow a little bit higher and make a beautiful new shape.

(Blow) You are now a little bit bigger.

(Blow) And a little bit bigger.

100

(Blow) And bigger.

(Blow) And bigger!

Freeze! Hold it! Does someone need more air?

I'm not satisfied that you all are as stretched tall and "full of air" as possible, so fill your arms with more air. And let me give you more air, and here's more for you and you and you and you.

Now we will make the balloons smaller again.

Listen for the sound of the air coming out of the balloon.

Get smaller only when you hear that sound.

Stop and freeze when the sound stops.

ADULT   A soft "ssss" sound will help the children to imagine the air seeping out of the balloon.

CHILDREN   Ssss—you are now a little bit smaller.

Ssss—and a little bit smaller.

Ssss—and smaller.

Ssss—and smaller!

You are flat on the floor. You have no more air inside of you.

ADULT   There will be some children with a shoulder or knee or neck that is still carrying some "air" (tension). As before, suggest that they let the air out of those specific parts and use the "ssss" sound to help them to feel the relaxation.

Bursting Balloon

WHAT YOUR CHILDREN WILL GAIN FROM THIS EXPERIENCE		
PHYSICAL / MUSICAL Body Control Spatial Awareness	COGNITIVE Problem Solving Ability to Organize Awareness of Shapes	EMOTIONAL / SOCIAL Self-Discipline Confidence Self-Esteem Imagination Responsibility to Group Group Responsibility to the Individual

ACCOMPANIMENT
"Listening Music" SIDE B, TRACK 2

■ You Need

Two completely different sounds. It makes no difference whether you use a musical instrument, a clap of your hands, or a pencil tapping on a table. The important thing is that you establish with the children at the start a particular sound to signal for the bursting of the balloon and another sound that signals the children to return to the group and to make a new balloon. We frequently bang on a drum for the bursting and we tap the side of the drum with a drumstick for the second sound that will make a new balloon.

You will need enough children to form a circle.

ADULT   As you talk, turn slowly checking the roundness of the circle. Help each child to become part of the round shape. Also, help the group to recognize that they need to clear enough space for each child. Keep turning as you blow out. Stop after each blow to check on the circle.

CHILDREN   I will stand in the middle. You make a circle around me. This is not just a circle, it is a round balloon!

Can you make it really round without holding hands?

Lower your arms. Come stand close together.

The balloon has to be small at first because I am going to blow you up. Let me see what happens when I blow just a little bit of air into this round balloon.

(Blow) You're getting bigger—keep it round.
(Blow) And bigger—watch the circle.
What will happen if I keep blowing?
That's right. The balloon will burst.

But you burst only when you hear this signal (give a bang or some other sound). And when the balloon bursts, each of you becomes a small piece of the balloon.

But do you know what? The balloon is sitting on the ocean! When you burst, all of the pieces start floating around. Float anywhere in the room.

Listen for the signal. Here we go, getting bigger.

(Blow) And bigger.

(Blow) And bigger.

(Bang the agreed-upon signal!) BURST!

Feel your body floating on the ocean. Feel the waves lifting you. They are making you lean and bend and turn. Have your arms float.

Listen for the second signal. Keep floating until you hear you it. (Give the second sound.) Float back to me and make a new balloon. Make it small enough so I can blow you up again.

ADULT   Repeat the game.

After you have been in the center blowing up the balloon at least twice, give the children turns. Remind each of them to turn slowly as they blow and to check the roundness of the circle. Giving them the opportunity to play the role of the teacher is a powerful source of confidence.

Music can be used for the floating section after the balloon has burst. The music will inspire the children to move more smoothly and lyrically.

Learning to Gallop

WHAT YOUR CHILDREN WILL GAIN FROM THIS EXPERIENCE		
PHYSICAL / MUSICAL	COGNITIVE	EMOTIONAL / SOCIAL
Body Control	Conscious Muscle	Handling Fear of
Coordination	Control	Leaving the Ground
Balance	Integration of Right &	Confidence
Use of Nondominant	Left Hemispheres of	Expressing Caring &
Side	the Brain	Tender Feelings
Coordinating Rhythm &		Imagination
Movement		Fun

ACCOMPANIMENT
"Learning to Gallop" SIDE B, TRACK 8

ADULT

Doing a gallop correctly is a difficult skill. We do not recommend teaching it to very young children.

Galloping requires the confidence to lift both feet off the ground almost simultaneously while you are progressing through space. It requires solving a complex motor skill and rhythmic problem. Start teaching it after age five but do not expect success until after age six.

Use the music right from the beginning, as you demonstrate the high lift of the knees.

When the children can hear and see the rhythm of the movement, they are more likely to pick it up.

Remind them to "Hold the reins. It helps them to stay focused, so that they can concentrate on the body techniques.

CHILDREN

Imagine that you are sitting on a horse.

You are very proud to be riding this beautiful horse.

106

Hold the reins with both hands in front of you.

Pull up tall in your back.

Now imagine that your legs are the horse's legs.
How does a horse move its legs when it is galloping?

That's right! Both knees come high up in front of
you—one right after the other. You are galloping!

Puppeteers

WHAT YOUR CHILDREN WILL GAIN FROM THIS EXPERIENCE		
PHYSICAL / MUSICAL *Relaxation* *Isolation and* *Articulation of Body* *Parts* *Coordination of* *Movement & Music* *Spatial Awareness*	**COGNITIVE** *Problem Solving* *Coordination of* *Movement &* *Language*	**EMOTIONAL / SOCIAL** *Concentration* *Listening Skills* *Observation Skills* *Attentiveness* *Focus* *Connecting with the* *Adult*

● You Need

A clean floor.

ADULT

Repeat the action a few times until you are fairly sure that the child understands that you are initiating and controlling the movement. While the child is focusing on your movement, her or his arm will relax.

The possibilities are endless—strings can be attached to the ankles (be careful to lower the heel gently), to the head (again, lower it carefully), to as many body parts as you choose.

The important goal is that the child remains intently focused on, and is connected to, the imaginary string.

CHILDREN

Lie on the floor on your back.

You are a marionette made of rags. You have no bones, no muscles.

I am a puppeteer tying a pretend string onto one wrist.

Show me what happens when I slowly pull up on the string.

Good. Now I will let your arm down gently.

Good. I'm tying another string on the other wrist. I'm lifting it up and letting it down.

Watch carefully—I can lift both arms at the same time. Then I can lower one while I lift the other.

I can circle the arm, now circle the other way.

● Partners

ACCOMPANIMENT
"Dancing Marionette" SIDE B, TRACK 3
"Listening Music" SIDE B, TRACK 2
"Greensleeves" SIDE B, TRACK 7

ADULT   The partners game will work best with your older groups. The amount of concentration that you can

expect will vary greatly with different individuals and with different groups.

If only one or two children out of a whole group are finding it too difficult to stay focused suggest that they watch for a while, but not together. You will notice that in the act of watching they are kinesthetically absorbing the purpose of the activity.

CHILDREN Everybody gets a partner. One person is now the puppet and the other person is the puppeteer.

Tie your imaginary string onto the puppet's wrist.

Do you remember how carefully and slowly I had to move so that my partner could feel the string?

● Variation

For your more mature students: Puppet and puppeteer duets that involve standing and moving can be created and performed for the group.

Let the children choose any of the three musical selections for their original duets.

Snowflakes

WHAT YOUR CHILDREN WILL GAIN FROM THIS EXPERIENCE		
PHYSICAL/MUSICAL Body Control Kinesthetic Memory Relaxation	COGNITIVE Awareness of Weight; Energy; Tempo; Shape; Sound; Gravity; Crystals	EMOTIONAL/SOCIAL Self-Discipline Stress Management Aesthetics Relaxation Self-Esteem

▲ You Need

Bare feet if possible.

CHILDREN   I wonder how it feels to be a snowflake.

Do you think it feels different from a raindrop?

How? Yes, it's lighter.

What else is different? Yes, it is not as wet.

Does it fall from the sky like a raindrop? No? Show me.

Does it make the same sounds?

Does it feel as strong and hard as a raindrop?

▲ Fingers

ACCOMPANIMENT
"Greensleeves" SIDE B, TRACK 7

ADULT   Add the music. Keep the music quietly in the background so that your voice can remain soft and hushed to create a magical atmosphere. Show me with your fingers, how soft and feathery and delicate a snowflake feels.

Using your fingers, show me how it starts high in the sky and floats down to the ground slowly and softly and quietly.

▲ Arms

ACCOMPANIMENT
"Greensleeves" SIDE B, TRACK 7

CHILDREN Now make your whole arm a snowflake.

You can have one arm at a time float. You can move one arm down while the other floats up.

Imagine a soft breeze that blows the snowflake to the side as it floats down.

Remember how soft it feels. Beautiful!

▲ Legs

ACCOMPANIMENT
"Greensleeves" SIDE B, TRACK 7

CHILDREN I wonder if your legs could feel so soft and light as your arms? It will be more difficult but let's try.

Sit on the floor. Place your hands behind you on the floor so you can balance.

Lift one leg. Start with just your toes. Feel one toe at a time getting softer and softer.

Now feel your whole foot soften and your ankle. Soften the muscles up to your knee.

Do you notice how your leg is being pulled downward?

It's called "gravity." The pull of gravity also brings down the snowflakes.

If you soften your toes and foot and leg, your leg will come down all by itself.

Now try the other leg.

▲ Total Body

ACCOMPANIMENT
"Greensleeves" SIDE B, TRACK 7

CHILDREN   Stand up. Your whole body is a snowflake. Feel your head and neck getting soft and feathery.

Feel a light breeze moving your head and neck very gently to one side and another.

Feel your shoulders getting soft. Let gravity pull them downward.

Now gravity is pulling your chest and your back, and your arms. Feel your whole body floating and gently being blown through space on the way down. Beautiful!

ADULT	Your lesson on snowflakes could end here, or you could continue if the children are old enough.
	Turn off the music while you talk about crystals.

▲ Crystals

	ACCOMPANIMENT
	A drumbeat or a hand clap can signal the children to change to another shape.

CHILDREN	I wonder if all snowflakes look the same?
	Has anyone of you seen—on television or through a microscope—what a snowflake looks like?
	The frozen shapes are called "crystals." They are beautiful shapes. And each one is different. Just like you. No one ever looks exactly like anyone else— even if you are twins.
	Imagine that you are a beautiful crystal. When I signal, make a shape with your body and freeze.
	Pretend that I am taking your picture—hold still while I snap each of you.
	While you are holding still, try to memorize your shape. Where are your arms? Your legs? Your back? Your head? Good! Now everyone melt slowly.
	Here's the signal—make a new shape with your body and freeze.

▲ Polaroid

ADULT	Call each child's name in turn and ask the children to remember the shape they had created when you snapped them.
	Let them take their time reconstructing the pose. Compliment them on the variety of levels, directions, and imaginative images.

CHILDREN I took your pictures with a pretend Polaroid camera. Now we will watch the photos develop.

Do you notice how different each shape is from another shape?

Everyone, take another shape and I'll take another picture.

S n o w S t a t u e s

WHAT YOUR CHILDREN WILL GAIN FROM THIS EXPERIENCE		
PHYSICAL / MUSICAL *Body Control* *Isolation of Body Parts* *Relaxation*	COGNITIVE *Naming Body Parts*	EMOTIONAL / SOCIAL *Imagination* *Relaxation* *Learning to be Gentle* *Fun*

■ Creating a Statue

ADULT   Clay can also be used as the image for this activity. Be aware that children pretending to be snow cannot be expected to hold frozen positions for long.

CHILDREN   Everybody gets a partner. One of you is the Snow, the other is the Sculptor.

SNOW   Lie down on the ground like a heap of snow. Try to feel as soft as snow.

When your partner moves one of your body parts, try to keep the rest of your body from moving.

Relax the part that is being moved as much as you can to make it easy for your partner to create a beautiful snow statue. Once you are positioned, though, try to freeze in that position.

SCULPTOR   Put on some pretend gloves so that your hands will not freeze as you create a snow statue.

Gently lift your partner's arm. Place it where you would like it to be.

Pat the snow carefully all around the arm to make it stay firm.

Now move your partner's head. Position it carefully and pat it very gently.

Now put your hands under your partner's shoulders and lift the body. Place it where you would like it to be and pat it gently.

Do you like the way your snow statue looks?

You can gently fix any part of the body: knees, mouth, fingers.

Carefully place each part into a position that you like best, then pat it gently.

SUN CHILD   The snow statue is now finished.

Turn yourself into the Sun Child.

Move your arms slowly. Make big, round circles.

Slowly walk or dance around the snow statue. While you shine your warm sun-arms onto it, turn your whole body very slowly. Feel round and warm and glowing.

Keep moving and shining, even when you notice the snow statue is melting.

SNOW   The snow statue stays frozen.

Let the Sun Child shine all around you before you begin to melt.

Melt only one part at a time. First your head starts to melt. You can feel the wet drops dripping down your nose.

Let your chin sink down to your chest.

Let each finger begin to melt, then your wrists, your elbows, your shoulders, your knees, your hips, your ankles, your toes.
Now it is your turn to make a statue!

■ Variation

The child pretending to be a statue can play the Sun Child as well but it's preferable that a third child join the game.

The children can create a short dance/pantomime with the three characters: Sculptor, Snow, Sun.

Trains and Stations

WHAT YOUR CHILDREN WILL GAIN FROM THIS EXPERIENCE		
PHYSICAL / MUSICAL Warm-Up Back Strength Stomach Muscle Strength Body Control Musical Phrasing Breath Control Relaxation	COGNITIVE Visual Awareness of Space Alertness Contrast	EMOTIONAL / SOCIAL Self-Discipline Stress Management Self-Esteem Fun Relaxation

ACCOMPANIMENT
"Trains and Stations" SIDE B, TRACK 9

● You Need

A clean, smooth floor with enough space for the single child moving alone or for a large group.

● Listening

CHILDREN   Sit near me.

When you listen to the music, you will hear train sounds. You will also hear sounds that tell you that the train has stopped moving. It has reached its station. The train is resting so that the engine can cool off.

When you can hear that the train is resting in the music, put up one hand.

Very good! I will play the music again.

ADULT	Play enough of the music to be sure that each child has heard the contrasting themes. Your nod of approval each time a child's hand goes up will encourage the process.
CHILDREN	This time, everyone make a little circle with your mouth like this—let me demonstrate. (Adult demonstrates.)
	Now without making a sound, very quietly blow air out through your mouth a little bit at a time. You only make the O shape when the train has stopped to rest. You are helping the engine to cool off.

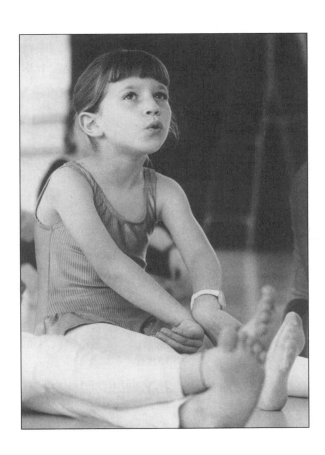

ADULT   This time, the children use the O-shaped breath
               movement rather than raising their hands. If you will
               do it with them, they will catch on quickly. As you
               exhale your breath gradually lower your shoulders
               and relax your arms down to your sides. The
               children will imitate you without your needing to talk
               about it.

● Train Music

ADULT   The older the children are, the more you can expect
               them to straighten their legs.

CHILDREN   Sit on the floor with your legs stretched in front of
               you. Keep your hands off the floor.

               You are the train.

               Travel forward by lifting one buttock at a time and
               stretching each leg forward in front of you.

               You have to try to travel in a straight line.

You can decide for yourself how far you want to go before you arrive at the station and the music changes to station music.

● Station Music

ADULT The very slow lowering of the body strengthens the children's stomach muscles (they do not have to reach the floor, however). At the same time, the exhaling of the breath is relaxing. **Be careful to avoid hyperventilation.**

CHILDREN I will count from one to five to make sure that the engine has lots of time to cool off. Make your O shape with the mouth.

Start blowing when I count and keep blowing until the count of five. As you blow out the air, gradually lower your body toward the floor. One, two, three, four, five!

● Train

CHILDREN Each time that you hear the train music, sit up and do the train movement. When you hear the station music, cool off the engine of the train.

ADULT Alternate the two themes of train and station music and activities, depending on your space, the age and size of your group, and how long you want the activity to continue. Watch for weariness.

● Variation

The train movement can also move backward. But when the children move backward, they will need to place their hands on the floor to help them keep their balance.

SPECIAL OFFER
"Goodnight Toes!" Cassette
and Other Dance Books

The authors have prepared a special cassette to accompany the dance games in **Goodnight Toes!** The tape includes folk, classical, and world music that will increase your enjoyment of the book. To order, fill out the order form on the back of this page.

Goodnight Toes! Cassette includes: All the Pretty Horses; Russian Lullabye; Pajamas; Goodnight Song; Sleep Songs; Hit the Road to Dreamland; Raisins and Almonds; Goodnight Toes!; Listening Music, Classical Style; Dancing Marionette; Learning to Skip; Sprightly Rhythms; Rhythm Game; Greensleeves; Learning to Gallop; Trains and Stations.   **Price: $9.95**

We also recommend the following titles:

Hello Toes! Movement Games for Children supplies enjoyable activities for parents and caregivers and children to increase coordination and creativity.   **Price $9.95**

Hello Toes! Cassette includes: Invisible Strings; Freeze & Move; Twirling; Jumping; Choo-choo; Sliding; Balloon Dance/Story; Bird in the Nest; Chay-Chay Koolay; Hello Toes; Shoo Lie Loo; Sleep Songs.   **Price: $9.95**

Playdancing: Discovering and Developing Creativity in Young Children is an innovative program that develops creativity with movement, music, drawing, writing, and dramatic play exercises.   **Price $12.95**

Towards Ballet: Dance Training for the Very Young by Beryl Manthorp. Dance games for children aged 2-5 years that develop posture, coordination, and movement control.   **Price: $10.95**

First Steps in Ballet by Thalia Mara. Beginning ballet exercises at the barre for students age 7 and up.   **Price: $6.95**

The Language of Ballet: A Dictionary by Thalia Mara. Basic terms and famous dancers and choreographers, written for children age 10 and up. **Price: $9.95**

To order, or to be added to our mailing list, please fill out the form on the back of this page.

ORDER FORM

Please send me:

- ☐ Goodnight Toes! Cassette $9.95
- ☐ Hello Toes! by Anne Lief Barlin and Nurit Kalev $9.95
- ☐ Hello Toes! Cassette $9.95
- ☐ Playdancing: Discovering and Developing Creativity in Young Children by Diane Lynch Fraser $12.95
- ☐ Towards Ballet: Dance Training for the Very Young by Beryl Manthorp $10.95
- ☐ First Steps in Ballet by Thalia Mara $6.95
- ☐ The Language of Ballet: A Dictionary by Thalia Mara $9.95

Name _____

Address _____

City _____ State _____ Zip _____

Day Phone _____

- ☐ My check or money order for $ _____ is enclosed.

- ☐ Please charge: ☐ Visa   ☐ MasterCard   ☐ American Express

Account Number _____ Exp Date _____

Signature _____

- ☐ Please send your FREE dance book and video catalog.

You may phone in your order from
8:30 - 4:30 Eastern time at our toll-free number
1-800-220-7149

Return this form with your payment to:
Princeton Book Company, Publishers
PO Box 57, Pennington, New Jersey 08534